HOW TO CONTROL YOUR EMOTIONS

IT'S NOT ALWAYS A BAD THING

IDOWU KOLAWOLE

TABLE OF CONTENT

Chapter 1

What does Emotions mean

Humans' reactions to events or circumstances, or their emotions, are known as emotions. The situation that causes an emotion determines the kind of feeling that an individual will feel. For instance, when someone hears excellent news, they are happy. When someone is in danger, they get afraid.

Emotions are the responses or feelings that people have to things or situations. The sort of emotion that a person will experience depends on the circumstance that triggers it. For example, when someone receives good news, they are joyful. People get fearful when they are in danger.

What Are Emotions?

In their book "Discovering Psychology," writers Don Hockenbury and Sandra E. Hockenbury propose that an inclination is a complex mental express that includes three unmistakable parts: an emotional encounter, a physiological reaction, and a conduct or expressive reaction.

As well as attempting to characterize what feelings are, specialists have likewise attempted to distinguish and group the various kinds of feelings. The depictions and bits of knowledge have changed over the long haul.

- In 1972, psychologist Paul Ekman proposed that there are six fundamental feelings that are general all through human societies: dread, disdain, outrage, shock, satisfaction, and sadness.

- During the 1980s, Robert Plutchik presented one more feeling characterization framework known as the "wheel of feelings." This model showed the way that various feelings can be joined or combined as one, much the manner in which a craftsman blends essential tones to make other colors.

• In 1999, Ekman extended his rundown to incorporate various other essential feelings, including humiliation, energy, disdain, disgrace, pride, fulfillment, and amusement.3

Plutchik proposed eight essential close to home aspects: bliss versus trouble, outrage versus dread, trust versus nausea, and shock versus expectation. These feelings can then be consolidated to make others (like happiness + anticipation = excitement).

Essentials of Emotions

To more readily comprehend what feelings are, how about we center around their three key components, known as the abstract insight, the physiological reaction, and the social reaction.

Abstract Experience

While specialists accept that there are various fundamental general feelings that are capable of individuals all around the world paying little heed to foundation or culture, analysts additionally accept that encountering feelings can be profoundly subjective. Consider outrage, for instance. Is all outrage something similar? Your own experience could go from gentle inconvenience to blinding fury.

While we have expansive names for feelings, for example, "irate," "miserable," or "cheerful," your own insight of these feelings might be significantly more multi-faceted, consequently emotional.

We additionally don't necessarily encounter unadulterated types of every inclination. Blended feelings over various occasions or circumstances in our lives are normal. When confronted with beginning a new position, you could feel both invigorated and apprehensive. Getting hitched or having a kid may be set apart by a wide assortment of feelings going from euphoria to uneasiness. These feelings could happen all the while, or you could feel them consistently.

Physiological Response

Assuming you've at any point felt your stomach sway from nervousness or your heart touch with dread, then you understand that feelings likewise cause solid physiological responses.

A large number of the physiological reactions you experience during an inclination, for example, sweat-soaked palms or a hustling heartbeat, are managed by the thoughtful sensory system, a part of the autonomic sensory system.

The autonomic sensory system controls compulsory body reactions, for example, blood stream and absorption. The thoughtful sensory system is accused of controlling the body's survival responses. While confronting a danger, these reactions consequently set up your body to escape from risk or face the danger head-on.

While early investigations of the physiology of feeling would in general zero in on these autonomic reactions, later examination plays designated the cerebrum's part in feelings.

Cerebrum examinations have shown that the amygdala, some portion of the limbic framework, assumes a significant part in feeling and dread in particular.

The actual amygdala is a small, almond-formed structure that has been connected to persuasive states like craving and thirst as well as memory and feeling. Scientists have utilized mind imaging to show that when individuals are shown undermining pictures, the amygdala becomes enacted. Harm to the amygdala has additionally been displayed to hinder the trepidation response.

Instructions to Prevent and an Amygdala Hijack

Social Response

The last part is maybe one that you are generally acquainted with — the real articulation of feeling. We invest a lot of energy deciphering the close to home articulations of individuals around us. Our capacity to precisely comprehend these articulations is attached to what clinicians call the capacity to understand people at their core, and these articulations have a significant impact in our general non-verbal communication.

Research recommends that numerous articulations are general, for example, a grin to show joy or a grimace to demonstrate trouble.

Sociocultural standards likewise assume a part by the way we express and decipher feelings. In Japan, for instance, individuals will generally cover showcases of dread or repugnance when a power figure is available. Individuals in the United States are bound to communicate pessimistic feelings both alone and within the sight of others, while individuals in Japan are bound to do as such while alone.

Are Emotional Expressions Universal?

Hypotheses of Emotion

Charles Darwin proposed the transformative hypothesis of feeling, which recommends that feelings are versatile to our current circumstance and work on our possibilities of endurance. For instance, feelings like love are versatile in light of the fact that they advance mating and multiplication. Feelings like apprehension protect us from predators.

The James-Lange hypothesis keeps up with the idea that our actual reactions are answerable for emotion. If somebody surprises you and yells, for example, your pulse increments. Your pulse increment makes you feel dread.

The facial-criticism hypothesis explains the James-Lange hypothesis. It proposes that active work impacts feeling — for example, assuming that you force a grin, you will feel more joyful than you would on the off chance that you didn't grin at all.

The Cannon-Bard hypothesis discredits the James-Lange hypothesis, stating that individuals experience profound and actual reactions at the equivalent time.

The Schachter-Singer hypothesis is a mental hypothesis of feeling that recommends our contemplations are really liable for emotions. Similar to this hypothesis is the mental evaluation hypothesis. It states that somebody should initially think prior to encountering an inclination. For example, your cerebrum passes judgment on a circumstance as compromising, and thus, you experience fear.

Types of Emotions

There are different hypotheses regarding the number of sorts of feelings people that experience. As referenced, analyst Paul Ekman laid out the accompanying six widespread emotions:

- Happiness: Many individuals take a stab at joy, as it is a charming inclination joined by a feeling of prosperity and fulfillment. Bliss is in many cases communicated by grinning or talking in a playful manner of speaking.

- Sadness: All of us experience trouble occasionally. Somebody could communicate misery by crying, being peaceful, and additionally pulling out from others. Types of bitterness incorporate pain, sadness, and frustration.

- Fear: Fear can increment pulse, cause hustling considerations, or trigger the instinctive reaction. It very well may be a response to genuine or saw dangers. Certain individuals partake in the adrenaline rush that goes with dread through watching frightening films, riding thrill rides, or skydiving.

- Disgust: Disgust can be set off by an actual encounter, like seeing or smelling decaying food, blood, or unfortunate cleanliness. Moral repugnance might happen when somebody sees someone else accomplishing something they view as improper or distasteful.

- Anger: Anger can be communicated with glaring, hollering, or fierce ways of behaving. Outrage can persuade you to make changes in your day-to-day existence, however you want to track down a sound outlet to communicate outrage so it doesn't truly hurt yourself or others.

- Surprise: Surprise can be wonderful or unsavory. You could open your mouth or heave when you're surprised.20 Surprise, similar to fear, can set off the survival reaction.

Emotions, Feelings, and Moods

In regular language, individuals frequently utilize the terms feelings, sentiments, and temperaments conversely, yet these terms really mean various things. An inclination is regularly very brief, yet serious. Feelings are likewise liable to have a clear and recognizable reason. For instance, in the wake of contradicting a companion over governmental issues, you could encounter outrage.

Feelings are responses to upgrades, yet sentiments are what we experience because of feelings. Sentiments are affected by our view of the circumstance, which is the reason a similar inclination can set off various sentiments among individuals encountering it.

Take the case of contradicting your companion. You could both leave the discussion having encountered the feeling of outrage.

Your annoyance could feel like dissatisfaction since you feel that your companion never pays attention to you when you talk. Your companion's displeasure, then again, could feel like desire since they feel you discover significantly more about the point than they do. Both of you have a similar inclination, however your sentiments are different in light of your different understandings.

A mind-set can be depicted as an impermanent profound state. Once in a while mind-sets are brought about by clear reasons — you could feel everything is turning out well for you this week, so you're feeling cheerful. Be that as it may, much of the time, recognizing the particular reason for a mood can be troublesome. For instance, you could discover yourself feeling melancholy for a few days with next to no unmistakable, recognizable reason.

On the off chance that you've been battling with low temperament or troublesome feelings, converse with a specialist or an emotional well-being expert about your interests. They can offer help, direction, and arrangements that can assist you with returning to feeling your best. You can see our National Helpline Database to investigate various assets that could be useful

Chapter 2

What Impacts Your Emotion Negatively and Positively

Impact of Sleep on Your Emotions

Rest assumes a vital part in human capability and perception, influencing learning, memory, actual recuperation, digestion, and resistance. The useful job of rest is irrefutable across species, and all the more as of late, research has uncovered the capability of staying in bed managing feeling. The connection between the two is proportional; rest is significant for mental and actual wellbeing while at the same time managing feeling assumes an essential part in diminishing the unfavorable impacts of profound weight on rest physiology.

How really does rest influence the handling of positive and negative boosts?

It is generally acknowledged that rest is firmly embroiled in the handling of everyday anxieties and feelings. Logical writing has shown how rest seems fundamental for our capacity to adapt to profound pressure in day-to-day existence. Rest misfortune and sleep deprivation have been found to influence profound reactivity and socialization. The impact of rest has been legitimate at different degrees of capability, like on the psychomotor, tangible engine, and mental levels; in any case, the profound impacts are less clear.

Nonetheless, by and large, the response to pessimistic inclination has been recorded to be essentially improved, while responses to positive occasions are frequently curbed. A lack of sleep investigation discovered that the reaction to positive improvements was quicker comparative with the reaction inspired from negative and unbiased boosts. Different examinations have verified this, showing that rest misfortune increases abstract reports of pressure, uneasiness, and outrage because of low-stress circumstances and increases impulsivity towards negative boosts. Strikingly, impulsivity is related to a forceful way of behaving - a propensity related to lack of sleep.

In another lack of sleep study, 33 members were liable to rehashed practical attractive reverberation imaging (fMRI) meetings to decide the impact of 42 hours of lack of sleep and after rest recuperation on cerebrum reactions and circadian musicality in 33 solid members. The outcomes showed members' sensations of close to home pain (negative effect) remained nearly stable during the main day, after the fact altogether demolishing after the first and second melatonin onsets in their circadian mood, which signs rest.

The disturbance or hardship of rest is both a side effect and a gamble factor for a few mental problems. In examinations with kids and youthful grown-ups, deficient rest has expanded episodes of disarray, outrage, and discouragement close to sensations of touchiness, animosity, and dissatisfaction. This happened in even just one evening of lack of sleep; subjects saw an expansion in psychopathology schools for tension, wretchedness, and distrustfulness. In this equivalent exploration bunch, lack of sleep was related with a diminished capacity to acknowledge fault.

What rest means for your emotions | Sleeping with Science, a TED series

The drawn-out impacts of lack of sleep on emotional well-being

Rest unsettling influences obstruct a feeling of prosperity and may influence the turn of events and prognostic results of emotional issues like gloom. Since both quick eye development (REM) and non-REM (NREM) rest assist with balancing close to home and persuasive drives, these two rest stages permit more prominent profound limits and adaptiveness during attentiveness. Solid rest fixes useful mind movement and versatile handling. The respectability of the average prefrontal cortex-amygdala associations is significant in feeling guideline processes. To be sure, one evening of lack of sleep sets off a 60% enhancement in the amygdala's reactivity to pessimistic pictures compared with a typical evening of rest inwardly.

One more fundamental part of guideline is the administrative activity of the chemical cortisol, which is engaged with the control of pressure and reactivity against feelings. Melatonin, which can direct the response of cortisol, is a wellspring of circadian aggravation and makes sense of the adjustment of close to home reactivity and change of the circadian cycle because of lack of sleep - which is a wellspring of profound dysregulation.

As well as the fuel of close to home reactivity and reactions to fear, rest can make a negative standpoint and expand degrees of uneasiness. Altogether, research shows that lack of sleep increments stress over future occasions, especially assuming subjects are inclined toward tension overall. In one such review, lack of sleep was found to increment expectant uneasiness. Mind sweeps of 18 solid youthful grown-ups noticing pictures containing sincerely upsetting or genuinely unbiased substance were utilized to set off expectant uneasiness. In front of these pictures, subjects, when very much refreshed and accordingly sleepless, were given obvious signals before every series of pictures to pass the feeling on to be evoked (unbiased, pessimistic, or all things considered). Cerebrum movement because of the expectant sign was more noteworthy when the members were sleepless compared with the all around rested state, and this was articulated in light of members holding up in dramatic expectation. These reactions were viewed as especially articulated in the amygdala and the isolated cortex. This was especially enhanced in subjects who were accounted for to be naturally restless. Clarifications for this distinction are credited to changes in the amygdala, the profound control place. Here, sleepless members show a 60% more elevated level of movement in this space comparative with the very much refreshed state. Additionally, lack of sleep has been found to disturb the association between the amygdala and the average prefrontal cortex - this region directs the amygdala capability. Lack of sleep makes the amygdala go overboard to negative boosts as it becomes detached from mind regions that ordinarily safe its reactions.

Rest misfortune is likewise connected with decreased compassion and close to home acknowledgment; consequently, unfortunate rest might diminish understanding between accomplices in a relationship, expanding the potential for struggle. Diminished compassion and empathic exactness are likewise connected with expanded degrees of miscommunication and expanded affinity to fight back during struggle. These impacts are connected to another finding; only one evening of rest misfortune disables critical thinking, compounding a powerlessness to determine struggle.

Rest misfortune compromises ideal viable working, influencing feeling age the capacity to control feelings and express them. The agreement is that getting a satisfactory measure of rest every night advances a further developed state of mind and wellbeing.

Impact of Thoughts on Your Emotions

Our thought process influences what we feel. Contemplations trigger feelings. Good contemplations can set off positive sentiment feelings and pessimistic considerations can set off feelings that outcome in us feeling terrible.

Saying this doesn't imply that all feelings that cause us to feel awful are off-base, or terrible in themselves. For instance, on the off chance that we have lost a friend or family member, we want to feel miserable. That is correct and normal.

However, feeling irate, miserable or unfortunate (or an entire host of different feelings) because of contemplations that are not sensible of the circumstance isn't the best thing to manage. Especially as long as possible.

Channel what enters our faculties

A model is watching the information. What stories are forthcoming in the information? The awful ones. The miserable ones. The terrifying ones. They catch individuals' eye and that is the thing the news source plans to do. They need watchers and they need to introduce the news in a manner that certainly stands out for quite a while.

Another model is investing energy with overly critical, angry, individual discussions in a slanderous, irate, or offending way. What contemplations will focus on this?

Assuming we permit our brains to be loaded up with unfortunate, revolting, furious and troubling messages, almost certainly, our considerations will be affected by that to some extent. While perhaps not right away, then, at that point, an eating regimen of such mental siege can incur significant damage over the long run.

A shortfall of supportive, steady and positive impact on our viewpoints vows to convey a truly hopeless point of view.

With the ascent of sorrow and tension, upsetting degrees of abusive behavior at home and self-destruction in our general public, it appears to be like any consideration given to dealing with our viewpoints is a positive methodology.

(Note: not the slightest bit am I proposing placing our heads in the sand and overlooking reality! I'm proposing a viewpoint of equilibrium and point of view.)

Might we at any point Choose our Thoughts and Emotions?

Indeed, by and large, we can.

With a wish to more readily deal with our outlook and emotional well-being, in addition to the right tool kit and direction, we can.

Furthermore, this, basically, is the reason and goal behind my reality as an outlook coach.

Having taken myself from somebody who had no information on the impact of contemplations on feelings, and being fairly a heap of uneasiness, I completely value the uncommon power this extraordinary data can have on an individual's life! Assuming you wish to find how to make your own universe of quiet, expanded lucidity, decreased pressure and better progress in all parts of your life, message Sonya Matthews today.

Impact of Words on Your Emotions

Words have power. Their significance solidifies discernments that shape our convictions, drive our way of behaving, and at last, make our reality. Their power emerges from our close to home reactions when we read, talk, or hear them. Simply give the signal "fire" while grilling, or in the work environment, or in a packed theater, and you'll get three totally unique, however strong close to home and fiery responses.

The Optimistic Life

Quantum material science some time in the past resolved that actual matter doesn't actually exist, that everything is only energy in various conditions of vibration. Nobel Prize winning physicist Werner Heisenberg once expressed, "Molecules or rudimentary particles themselves are not genuine; they structure a universe of possibilities or potential outcomes, as opposed to one of things or realities." This energy vibrates at a limitless number of unpretentious frequencies that make it show up as every one of the various manifestations we find in our reality. There has been a lot of exploration lately concerning whether the universe we live in is really a holographic encounter, and it appears to be that this is exceptionally near reality.

Thus, it appears life is a greater amount of an energy stream than an assortment of strong things. How that affects us is that assuming we stay aware of the energy we contain, in light of the feelings we believe, we can settle on purposeful decisions that change our recurrence and make the real factors we want. Assuming that we're having a down outlook on something, we can decide to rethink what is happening and raise our own spirits. With a recharged viewpoint and a higher, more certain enthusiastic vibration, we have a greatly improved possibility of bringing great into our lives, as opposed to harshly rehashing old mix-ups.

Words are very integral assets that we can use to elevate our own energy and work on our lives, however we're frequently not aware of the words we express, read, and open ourselves to. Indeed, even the expressions of others can without much of a stretch influence our own vibration. Put in no time flat with a persistent whiner who utilizes a wide range of pessimistic terms, and you'll feel your own energy base out. Words have incredible power, so pick them (and your companions) admirably!

Words and Water

Japanese researcher, Masaru Emoto played out the absolute most captivating analyses on the impact that words have on energy in the 1990's. When frozen, water that is liberated from all debasements will frame delightful ice precious stones that closely resemble snowflakes under a magnifying lens. Water that is dirtied, or has added substances like fluoride, will freeze without framing gems. In his examinations, Emoto emptied unadulterated water into vials named with negative expressions like "I can't stand you" or "dread." After 24 hours, the water was frozen, and presently not solidified under the magnifying lens: It yielded dim, deformed clusters rather than wonderful trim like gems. Conversely, Emoto put marks that made statements like "I Love You," or "Harmony" on vials of dirtied water, and following 24 hours, they delivered sparkling, entirely hexagonal gems. Emoto's examinations demonstrated that energy produced by certain or negative words can really change the actual design of an article. The consequences of his examinations were nitty gritty in a progression of books starting with The Hidden Messages in Water, where you can see the dumbfounding photographs of these mind-blowing water gems.

The Impact of Thanksgiving

In another trial, Emoto tried the force of expressed words. He put two cups of cooked white rice in two separate bricklayer jolts and fixed the covers set up, marking one container "Much obliged" and the other, "You Fool." The containers were left in a primary school homeroom, and the understudies were told to express the words on the names to the comparing containers two times every day. Following 30 days, the rice in the container that was continually offended had withered into a dark, coagulated mass. The rice in the container that was said thanks to was however white and fleecy as the day it might have been made. This sensational illustration of the force of words is likewise itemized in Emoto's books.

Discard Words

How often a day do we discard our words? We make statements like, "I can't stand my hair," "I'm so moronic," "I'm such a clumsy person." We never feel that these words bring pessimistic energy into our vibration and influence us on an actual level, yet they do. Emoto's trials were led with water. Why? Since sound vibration goes through water multiple times quicker than it in all actuality does through outside. Consider the way that your body is more than 70% water and you'll comprehend how rapidly the vibration from negative words resounds in your cells. Antiquated sacred texts let us know that life and passing are in the force of the tongue. For reasons unknown, that is not a representation.

Say It Once More

A few of us are prone to utilize similar negative words again and again without much forethought. The issue is that the more we hear, read, or express a word or expression, the more power it has over us. This is on the grounds that the mind utilizes redundancy to pick up, looking for examples and consistency as a method for getting a handle on our general surroundings. Solely after being stated a couple of times might, we at any point comprehend that fire is consistently hot. You may not recollect the specific end date of the Civil War, yet chances are you actually understand what 8 x 9 is on the grounds that you needed to rehash your duplication tables again and again, penetrating it into your awareness. I'm certain you've encountered having a tune latched onto your subconscious mind the entire day, and attempt as you would, you can't get the song somewhere far away from me. Redundancy is the most integral asset to engrave something into our brains and keep it there.

This is of specific concern when we consider a peculiarity called the Illusion of Truth Effect. It fundamentally demonstrates that any assertion we read, see, or talk routinely is viewed as more substantial than one we're presented to just sporadically. Incredibly, it has no effect whether the data is valid or misleading. The main thing that matters is the manner by which we're frequently presented to it. Research from the University of California at Santa Barbara obviously shows that a powerless message rehashed two times turns out to be more substantial than a solid message heard just a single time. Indeed, even one reiteration has the ability to adjust our perspectives. The equivalent goes for pictures, which are simply considerations and thoughts amassed into a picture. Redundancy expands our psychological approval of anything we're presented to, which is the reason it functions admirably in political promulgation.

In the event that we're not completely aware of what we're presenting ourselves to, consistency will be the best truth like clockwork. Presently consider how frequently you've dishonestly called yourself moronic, unskilled, monstrous, or whatever else, and you start to comprehend how your inside misleading publicity shapes a bogus mental self-portrait.

1. Making Words Work.

To intentionally tackle the force of words for your advantage, begin with the ones you're utilizing.

2. No Name-Calling or Self-Criticism.

Everybody is doing all that can be expected at any second in time with the awareness they need to work with, including you. Be thoughtful and offer yourself a similar sympathy and empathy you'd stretch out to any other person.

3. Shut down All Self-Deprecation.

Never make your body, or something you've achieved, or whatever else in your life the object of a joke. Words have power, and quantum energy doesn't have a funny bone.

4. Oppose Gossiping and Speaking Ill of Others.

It's unimaginable for your words to reverberate in any other person's body yet your own.

5. Go on a Negativity Diet.

Rather than saying that dinner was horrendous, say, "I'd be wise to." You've essentially expressed whatever you might be thinking without investing negative effort through your body — you even utilized a positive word to make it happen!

6. Help the Positive Energy of Words.

Rather than expressing something like you lived it up at a show, increase the positive energy by saying perfect, breathtaking, or phenomenal, all things being equal. This vibe is much better and creates a greater vigorous reaction in the body.

7. Assuming you have some negative nancy in your friend network,

limit the time you enjoy with them or track down better companions. Negative energy has an approach to hauling everything encompassing it in, similar to a major dark opening. Keep away from it when you can.

8. Encircle yourself with positive, inspiring words.

Put attestations on sticky notes around your home and office that express magnificent things about you, your family, or your objectives. Wear garments that have positive messages or expressions on them. Envision the sort of sure energy you'll create for yourself while you're wearing inspiration the entire day. As you continue to do these things, you utilize the force of reiteration in an exceptionally successful manner for your advantage. You have the ability to influence your reality, and utilizing words intentionally is one of the fastest ways of moving the energy you bring into your life.

Impact of Music on Your Emotions

Your life is impacted by music in a variety of ways.

What's fascinating about music is that you are being drenched in it constantly, once in a while without you in any event, mulling over everything. It's far beyond turning on the radio or paying attention to your #1 playlist; music likewise exists in your number one network shows/motion pictures, while you're sitting in an eatery, moving at the club and in any event, while chilling with your #1 web-based games.

Music is surrounding you and continuously influencing your feelings - in any event, when you're not really mulling over everything or searching out a tune to play. Truth be told, even that delicate ambient sound, or the audio cues and music in your number one games will bring out feelings.

Support Your Level of Happiness

While music can influence you in various ways, it is an individual's joy level that changes. Did you have at least some idea that music of any kind - even miserable music - can wind up helping your state of mind? A review was directed in the UK by Durham University related to the University of Jyväskylä which showed even "miserable" music can support your satisfaction level. Concentrate on members' announced expanded degrees of solace and joy while paying attention to the music.

Music Acts as Stress Relief

Another way that music can influence your feelings connects with pressure. Feeling anxious is something that nearly everybody can connect with, whether it is infrequent pressure or persistent pressure. While there are numerous ways of combating pressure, music has demonstrated to be quite possibly the best strategy. A type of treatment makes no bad side impacts, and that implies you get pressure help without stressing over what you surrender in return.

Not persuaded it works? The following time you feel worried, take a stab at paying attention to your top choices tunes for some time. There's a decent opportunity that pressure begins to drift away or possibly decrease.

It Can Evoke Memories

There's likewise the way that a specific tune, craftsman or sound can summon recollections. Presently, this can go the two different ways as it could be a positive or negative memory, however that tune can in a flash carry the memory to mind, consequently making a surge of feelings. Maybe it helps you to remember a get-away, a unique dance you imparted to somebody, a festival or occasion, etc.

Getting Down to the Science

Yet, what is the real logical side of what music means for your feelings? While standing by listening to music, it can deliver dopamine. This is many times depicted as an all-normal stimulant. Thus, you can then begin to group paying attention to music as a type of treatment. It is making a tactile excitement that your body responds to intellectually and genuinely. To finish it off, this response is practically prompt, so there's no caution required.

On the off chance that you're experiencing pressure and are precisely unsettled and cheery lately, you might need to ponder adding more music to your day-to-day existence. In any event, it will be a fascinating trial to perceive how your feelings change and respond.

Chapter 3

How to Alter Your Emotions

Sooner or later in time, everybody has encountered a scope of feelings: both good and pessimistic. Tragically, individuals wish to get a handle on their feelings yet turn out to be constrained by similar feelings. Somebody could fly off the handle, apprehensive, or blow their top and wind up causing more implosion or damage. Feelings resemble cautioning signs. For example, feeling furious is an indication that something wrong is occurring. In this article, we'll investigate the kinds of feelings, the viability of controlling your feelings, and eventually how to get a handle on your feelings.

Advantages of Controlling Your Emotions

There are many advantages related with controlling feelings as follows:

1. You'll figure out the reason for feelings

One of the advantages when you control your feelings, is that you give yourself an additional opportunity to comprehend the reason why you're encountering them in any case. For instance, assuming you shun exploding angrily when somebody harms you when you step back and consider it, you could see that you were disappointed with something that happened before in the day and not frantic at anybody specifically.

2. Request help to get a handle on your feelings

At the point when you know how to get a grip on your feelings, you're bound to know when you really want to request help. For instance, on the off chance that you're encountering a ton of dread because of PTSD, you could step back and tell yourself, “It appears as though now is the right time to converse with a psychologist." When you're mindful of your feelings, you know when you're in too far. Furthermore, you possibly become mindful of your sentiments when you know how to get a grip on your feelings.

3. Forestall the unfriendly impacts of gloomy feelings

Have you at any point responded ineffectively because of suppressed feelings? Simply sit back and relax, we as a whole have. Controlling your feelings is tied in with seeing them, believing them, and allowing them to drift away. At the point when we offer our pessimistic feelings consideration as opposed to responding to them, we can save ourselves from a lot of hopelessness.

4. You'll be a superior companion or accomplice by controlling your feelings

Individuals who know how to get a grip on their feelings can uphold individuals when they respond adversely. For instance, in the event that somebody lashes out at you, you could express something like, "You appear to be furious at the present time; what might I do for you to settle what is happening and facilitate your feelings of anxiety?" Saying something like this would quickly cut the pressure as opposed to responding to somebody's annoyance with more resentment.

5. You'll try not to consume undesirable substances

Frequently, when we neglect to get a handle on our feelings, we resort to gorging, liquor, drugs, or different substances that deteriorate our concerns. At the point when you control your sentiments, you're ready to rehearse careful eating and other solid ways of life.

6. Legitimate correspondence won't be a test

At the point when individuals have the instruments that improve dealing with their feelings, they're better ready to impart when difficulties emerge. Assuming you're at present battling with this, you should look at correspondence books like Nonviolent Communication by Marshall B. Rosenberg.

Step by step instructions to get a handle on your emotions

Before you even comprehend how to get a grip on your feelings, it's fundamental to realize which feelings you consistently experience and their conceivable result. The following are a few top ways for controlling your feelings:

1. Recognize your emotions

The most vital phase in managing your feelings is to recognize your ongoing inclination about the circumstance. Keep in mind, you can't oversee what you don't have any idea. It's fundamental to comprehend assuming you're overcompensating to an issue so you can do whatever it takes to begin feeling the board cycle. Whether or not you're miserable, apprehensive, disheartened, or furious, you could wind up hurting yourself or others.

Once in a while, you could encounter different feelings that can impact your direction. Recognizing your sentiments will assist you with understanding what you're managing right now to come by the best results. Additionally, by recognizing your sentiments, you become mindful of them. Assuming you're always unable to see them surfacing, you will not have the option to stop the blasts of feeling or eruptions.

2. Taking care of oneself is critical to getting a grip on your emotions

At times, your feelings can emerge from variables like life difficulties, stress, being separated from everyone else, or even not getting sufficient profound rest. This large number of elements have an immediate connection with human feelings. Thus, it's vital for training that taking care of oneself is really important for your general prosperity.

Mental examinations show that rest assumes a basic part in the prosperity of an individual. Inability to rest soundly for eight hours will segregate you from your feelings in light of the fact that your drained mind can't go with the most ideal choices. Then again, you probably won't get satisfactory rest due to gloomy feelings leading to additional issues. A comparable cycle is additionally engaged with different perspectives like pressure. To forestall these and better control your feelings, discover a few ideal exercises and make them an everyday practice.

For example, making some night memories standard, like working out, showering, and perusing before bed, can assist you with loosening up around evening time so you can get the rest you want. Additionally, having right-cerebrum exercises like drawing, playing music, or different exercises can likewise assist with hushing negative considerations to limit going overboard to minor issues.

3. Change your contemplations to deal with your emotions

Feelings have a huge impact in how individuals see various things. For example, in a work environment setting, getting restless once in a while is ordinary. For this situation, assuming by any opportunity you're called by your chief, you'll imagine that you're in a difficult situation assuming this is uncommon. Reexamining your considerations will cause you to have a practical perspective on various circumstances.

Pessimistic reasoning is generally the reason for gloomy feelings. Whenever you wind up thinking adversely, center around doing positive activities. You can do exercises like swimming, strolling, thinking, drawing, utilizing care diaries, or running.

4. Record what you're encountering

Making a state of mind diary is fundamental if you have any desire to really deal with your feelings. You ought to get a piece of paper and a pen and begin composing how you feel everyday, what feelings have meant for you, and what's going on in life overall.

At times, you could wind up in a place where you can't comprehend how or why you feel a specific way. You could confront a troublesome time expounding on your ongoing circumstance, particularly on the off chance that you can't yet get a grip on your feelings. For this situation, you ought to attempt to relate the inclination with another comparable circumstance you've recently had.

To make it much simpler, you ought to utilize diary prompts or brain maps that include making little air pockets and filling them with your viewpoints. At the top, start with the more extensive point and add subtopics a while later.

5. Keep solid connections

Connections assume a huge part with regards to close to home control. Connections are fundamental for managing feelings, so you can keep up with them. While you're feeling furious or unpleasant, conversing with your dear companion, relative, or accomplice can cheer you up. You'll get inner harmony in the wake of getting the basic reassurance that will likewise quiet your actual reaction.

Moreover, it's additionally indispensable to keep up close bonds with a portion of your companions to open up at whatever point you face testing or unpleasant circumstances that you can't impart to everybody. To keep these nearby ties, guarantee you're in normal contact with these individuals either genuinely, in outside exercises, or through web-based entertainment or text.

6. Give yourself space

In spite of the fact that being separated from everyone else over and over again is certainly not a smart thought for individuals attempting to deal with their feelings, it's useful for other people. You ought to give yourself some space in some cases. Along these lines, you'll figure out your sentiments undisturbed until you feel far improved. Giving yourself space likewise implies that you'll possess sufficient energy for conceptualizing your real sentiments and begin the method involved with attempting to gradually oversee them.

Moving away from individuals or issues assists you with figuring out how to get a grip on your feelings. You can get internal harmony from these minutes alone, so know when now is the ideal time to take them. Assuming the contention is in your marriage or long-haul relationship, don't stall the other individual. All things being equal, say, "I need to carry my best self to this issue we're managing. Is it OK in the event that I require thirty minutes to chill alone so we can determine this together?"

7. Stay away from triggers to assist you with controlling your emotions

All feelings have explicit triggers. Subsequently, to effortlessly get a grip on your feelings, you should initially distinguish the triggers and avoid them. For example, in the event that you feel furious and disheartened when you're not valued, you ought to attempt to stay away from those conditions and circumstances you think could cause a slight. This strategy normally functions admirably for gloomy feelings.

An amazing method for managing triggers in your connections is to portray the way in which you feel about something that irritates you with the individual who triggers you.

8. Search for mind-set promoters

Having a terrible state of mind will set off feelings that will hold you down. You'll likewise be in an unfortunate perspective where you're probably going to gripe a ton, remain on your telephone for extended periods or participate in harmful ways of behaving. It's subsequently fundamental to embrace the beneficial routines that will make an extremely durable shift of your mind-set from most exceedingly terrible to better.

The exercises you pick don't need to be too extraordinary for this situation. For example, rather than looking over your telephone the entire day, you can contact your companions, have some good times and happy discussions, pay attention to your #1 music, or contemplate.

9. Utilizing Meditation to get a handle on your feelings

Reflection is a brilliant answer for managing outrageous feelings and sentiments. Many individuals have as of late gone to contemplation for the vast majority different reasons, including better and quality rest and unwinding.

Chapter 4

How to develop emotionally

Whether it relates to your connections, profession, or your very own prosperity, knowing how to intensely through whimsical circumstances by observing ways of being major areas of strength for sincerely emphatically impact your life. With regards to pressure, it can influence many individuals in various ways: some could cry each time they're baffled (blameworthy!) while others become peaceful and stow away until they feel far improved. While nothing bad can be said about both of those circumstances, knowing how to deal with your feelings and direct why you're feeling them can assist you with understanding yourself much better so you quit viewing yourself as frail.

"Close to home strength comes from permitting yourself to be both free and subordinate. This implies developing your inside assets and becoming open to looking for and tolerating help," says psychotherapist and creator Karen R.

Koenig M.Ed., L.C.S.W., in a meeting with Bustle over email.

Figuring out how to adapt to life's hardships is an incredible method for developing your profound fortitude. The following are 11 different ways you can make yourself genuinely impressive.

1. Honor the Strength of Your Past

It tends to be difficult to have serious areas of strength for genuinely you continue to live previously. You must expend those considerations and acknowledge the way that those battles made you who you are today — which are areas of strength for an individual. "Commonly we have harshness from the holocaust, subjection or even family 'customs' of misuse. We can all things being equal, honor the battles and our societies in a manner that is positive. Try not to limit the battle, yet perceive how it very well may be a method for regarding the strength from quite a while ago. On the off chance that we can respect the strength of the past, we are a consequence of that past, so we honor ourselves and become more grounded," says harmony psychotherapist and neuromarketing tactician Michele Paiva in a meeting with Bustle over email.

2. Go with Healthy Decisions

The vast majority of your profound strength for the most part comes from the inside. That implies you'll in all probability feel your best assuming you practice good eating habits and treat your body with care. "Realize that each time you pursue solid decisions, you reinforce yourself. Did you pick an apple over a treat; one point for strength! Did you go for a stroll and partake in the view? One more score for flexibility. Honor each time you do wellbeing," says Paiva.

3. Help other people In Need

It sounds unusual to help others while you're attempting to get a decent grip on things. However, when you're unselfish, you can have serious areas of strength to become the consideration you show for others can reverberate and spill into really focusing on your own life, as well. "Helping other people assemble compassion and sympathy improves us individuals, period. That forms flexibility," says Paiva.

4. Grin and Laugh More

For my self's purposes, there could be no more prominent inclination than really laughing uncontrollably. It's an incredible way for somebody to flood their framework with blissful chemicals and cheer them up while they're feeling down. Select to watch an entertaining film, or timetable more dates with individuals that lift you up. The more you participate in this sort of way of life, the better you might feel. "Giggling from an unadulterated spot (not mockery) assists with fortifying your lungs, heart, feelings and brings individuals toward you as opposed to away; an emotionally supportive network loaded up with grins is a magnificent method for expanding flexibility," says Paiva.

5. Embrace Your Adversities

Try not to pummel yourself when things don't turn out well for you. Falling flat is a piece of life and how you decide to challenge and acknowledge it can really modify your viewpoint in a positive manner. "Practice positive brain science and start to embrace your difficulties as a whole and misfortunes as your most noteworthy educators and powers for change," says all-encompassing health mentor Pax Tandon in a meeting with Bustle over email.

6. Express Your Emotions

On the off chance that you're feeling down, don't accept that as an indication of shortcoming. Rather than shielding your feelings, embrace them for what they are."Whether it's crying tears or shouting into a cushion, giving yourself the opportunity to express and consent to be human will make you more grounded from the back to front," says Tandon.

7. Search for Patterns in Your Behavior

"Do you generally wind up feeling like a casualty? Pick genuinely undesirable companions or sweethearts and hence end up troubled? Damage your triumphs and accomplishments? Think you need to be separated from everyone else, then disdain it?" expresses Koenig about searching for designs in your way of behaving. Whether you feel like a casualty when something turns out badly or you patronize yourself when you goof, look at these circumstances and sort out why you do and feel these things to fix these feelings and make areas of strength for yourself.

8. Quit Judging Yourself

"Quit making a decision about yourself. Lead with self-sympathy and interest in why you have specific contemplations and sentiments and why you participate in unambiguous ways of behaving," says Koenig. Embrace your feelings for what they are and don't attempt to close them out when you feel them. You would rather not take part in regrettable self-talk since it can aggravate you about yourself.

9. Face Emotional Challenges

The more you put yourself out there, the more grounded you might turn into. You need to practice your feelings regardless of whether it causes you to feel somewhat awkward. "Face personal challenges that are reasonable to place yourself in circumstances that make you somewhat awkward, however that might end up being useful to you develop inwardly," says Koenig.

10. Perceive Your Emotions

Try not to recuse yourself for having specific sentiments. It's normal to feel down, furious or even envious. While you're encountering any gloomy feelings, nicely look at them and figure what you maintain that your subsequent stage should be. "Permit yourself to perceive and acknowledge each feeling you have and afterward choose if you have any desire to seek after this inclination or let it go," Koenig says regarding perceiving your feelings.

11. Converse with A Therapist

"Going into treatment, regardless of whether it's for just a brief timeframe, can be an extraordinary method for taking care of on your close to home problems and internal strength level," says psychotherapist and creator of Your Best Age is Now Robi Ludwig in a meeting with Bustle over email. Try not to feel that going to see a specialist is something terrible. Expressing your concerns to somebody is an extraordinary method for sorting out why you're feeling a specific way so you can develop your profound fortitude.

Permit your solidarity to come from the inside, whether that implies you converse with a specialist or keep a sound way of life. Embrace your feelings for what they are and before long you'll become close to areas of strength for home.

Chapter 5

The Psychological Core

People are normally muddled. Feelings, contemplations, expectations, and information are only a couple of the boundless developments that make us, us. Through various styles of discipline (contemplations or yoga) we can completely recognize and communicate with 'ourselves'. The more obviously and exhaustive we are in distinguishing developments, the more productively we develop, both profoundly and intellectually.

There is a gathering of center developments that we will call focuses in this article. These focuses are like chakras yet to you.

The Security Center

This is simply the part that handles getting and safeguarding your essential requirements and wellbeing. Food, cover, water, family, companions, and general profound substance, are only a couple of instances of the resources that this part of yourself focuses on. Filling in as a kind of 'circumstance room', this viewpoint gets going when undermined or a need is distinguishing.

The Sensory Center

This piece of yourself is worried about your pleasure in life's wealth. This piece of you attempts to energize however many pleasurable exercises as it can. On the other side of that tangible coin, it tries to not be harmed.

The Power Center

Worried about both interior and outer types of force, this viewpoint looks for and will in general power. Creating wellsprings of financial stability, impact, and esteem, to acquire something very similar or taking a stab at a particular objective, you'll need to be cautious while supporting this middle. It's critical to have the option to impact our general surroundings as diverse as could be expected. Similarly, as significant, is modesty and a longing to reinforce your local area. To be careful from the avarice that drives individuals to do awful things for cash and power, absolutely never look for impact and power alone. These perspectives ought to possibly be looked for when a particular objective is perceived. After the objective has been done, stop controlling your current circumstance.

The Love Center

This middle is clearly liable for your close connections. The obligations of this middle reach out past that, including any relational connections, and the vital capacity to cherish ourselves. The advancement of this middle is essential to rising above the hindrances that different people from people. As you sustain this middle, you reinforce the info and result of your heart. This outcomes in a lift to the earnestness and recurrence of empathic reactions.

The Cornucopia Center

This genuinely determined part of yourself is answerable for the creation and upkeep of your feeling of cognizance and your specific impression of the real world.

The Self Awareness Center

This focal point of yours, is seemingly the main on this rundown, your mindfulness place will coordinate your character assets to all the more likely grasp yourself and your general surroundings. This included viewpoint is specific to you, so you'll need to continuously carve out opportunities to comprehend your inclination towards life and the connection between your sentiments and your development and efficiency rate.

The Cosmic Awareness Center

The infinite mindfulness community is the manner by which all your different focuses, gifts, companions and understandings bubble into the 'fantastic plan'. This is the most elevated functional place for you. When everything is terminating accurately with your different focuses, this will be where you focus on the secrets and endless excellence of the universe. This is where you set to the side 'you', your name and become one with the universe.

www.ingramcontent.com/pod-product-compliance
Lightning Source LLC
LaVergne TN
LVHW050342160826
845677LV00014B/3749

* 9 7 9 8 8 4 8 1 6 2 1 7 2 *